Truly Foul & Cheesy™

Revolting Records Facts

& Jokes

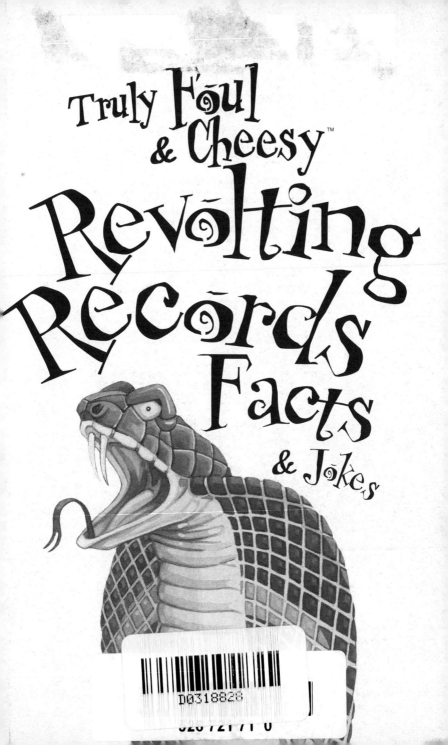

Published in Great Britain in MMXVIII by
Book House, an imprint of
The Salariya Book Company Ltd
25 Marlborough Place, Brighton BN1 1UB
www.salariya.com

ISBN: 978-1-912006-36-6

SALARIYA

1 3 5 7 9 8 6 4 2

A CIP catalogue record for this book is available
from the British Library.

Printed and bound in China.
Printed on paper from sustainable sources.

Created and designed by
David Salariya.

Visit
www.salariya.com
for our online catalogue and
free fun stuff.

PAPER FROM
SUSTAINABLE
FORESTS

Author:
John Townsend worked as a
secondary school teacher before
becoming a full-time writer.
He specialises in illuminating and
humorous information books for
all ages.

Artist:
David Antram studied at
Eastbourne College of Art and then
worked in advertising for 15 years
before becoming a full-time artist.
He has illustrated many children's
non-fiction books.

Truly Foul & Cheesy™
Revolting Records Facts
& Jokes

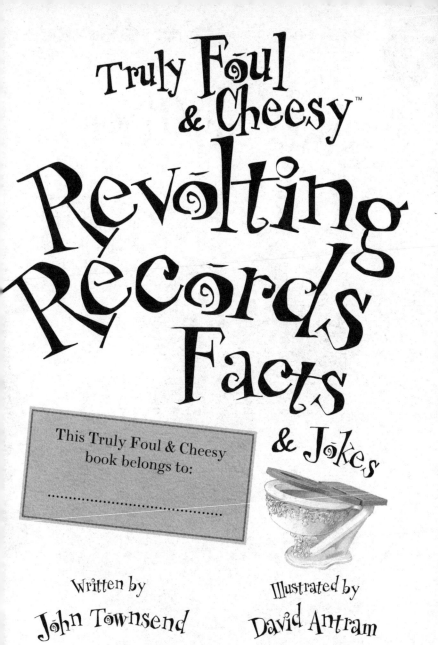

This Truly Foul & Cheesy book belongs to:

....

Written by
John Townsend

Illustrated by
David Antram

BOOK HOUSE
a SALARIYA imprint

Introduction

A little bird told me this book is REVOLTING.

Warning – reading this book might not make you LOL (laugh out loud) but it could make you GOL (groan out loud), feel sick out loud or SEL (scream even louder). If you are reading this in a library by a SILENCE sign... get ready to be thrown out!

Disclaimer: The author really hasn't made anything up in this book (apart from some daft limericks and jokes). He checked out the foul facts as best he could and even double-checked the fouler bits to make sure – so please don't get too upset if you find out something different or meet a world expert, total genius or a revolting record collector who happens to know better.

'If I had my way, I'd RATIfy the lot!'

official

warning

This book contains some of the weirdest, strangest, grossest and silliest details and events recorded. They appear in record books from today or were set down in historical records long ago. So, if you're on the look-out for some of the daftest, smelliest, vilest, unluckiest, slimiest, scariest, foulest, yuckiest and most ridiculous record-breakers, you're about to find them. If you're a bit squeamish or easily disgusted… look away now!

Revolting limerick

If you don't mind when things
get insulting
With plenty of gross stuff
resulting,
This book is for you,
With foul facts and all true,
Full of records that get so
REVOLTING!

Historical Records

Many revolting events have been recorded through history so a look back at a few grisly deaths might start you groaning and squealing. Some famous people from the past met their end in unusual and unexpected ways. Get ready to be amazed by these TOP TEN foul and cheesy deaths...

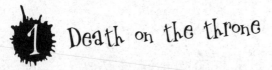 Death on the throne

King Edmund II, known as Edmund Ironside, was king of England in 1016. His short rule of about 7 months could have lasted many happy years had he not needed the toilet on his travels. The story goes that Edmund had to leave a battle and use one of the latrines perched over a ditch. Little did he know that a Viking was hiding below with a long sharp spear.

Just as Edmund lowered himself onto the toilet, the Viking stabbed the king twice up the bottom. What a way to GO! King Edmund II died there and then 'on the throne'. Maybe he should have worn iron underpants and been called Edmund Iron-underside. Now he's not so much known as Edmund Ironside as Edmund Up-the-Backside.

OUCH!

2 Death by Chuckles

A king of Sicily, known as Martin of Aragon, was killed by a joke. In 1401 he'd just eaten a whole goose (something kings often did) but it gave him a bout of nasty indigestion (and probably a few goose-bumps). So, he went up to his bedroom and called for his jester to come and cheer him up with a funny joke. No, it wasn't the riddle about a goose:

Q: Why couldn't the king see the goose fly?
A: Because it was in de skies (disguise).

No, it was an even worse joke about a deer hanging by its tail from a tree after eating figs (it was probably hilarious the way he told it). Anyway, Martin found this joke to be so funny, that he laughed uncontrollably for three hours, eventually falling out of bed. When he hit the floor, he was dead. Ah well, he died burping but happy.

3 Death by beard

AAAAAAAAAAHHHH!

The year was 1567 when a mayor in Bavaria (now Austria) was killed by his own beard. There are two versions of how his long beard (almost one and a half metres long) killed him. One story tells how Hans Steininger forgot to roll up his beard into a leather pouch so he tripped over it, broke his neck and killed himself. Another story tells how Steininger forgot to roll up his beard when he went to bed and a candle caught it alight. Either way, his beard killed him and it was more than a close shave.

4 Death by moustache (or burst bladder)

Being too polite to ask to 'be excused' isn't healthy. A famous Danish astronomer failed to go to the bathroom and it all ended horribly. Tycho Brahe (1546-1601) was extraordinary as he had no telescope but worked out the positions of many stars and comets. Weirdly, he also had a tame elk and a fake nose (he'd lost his own in a duel – as you do).

Brahe enjoyed plenty of banquets but his last one killed him because he drank a lot but felt it was impolite to leave the table to visit the toilet. Eventually it seems his bladder burst and it took eleven days for him to die of poisoning. At least, that's the official story. It's possible he actually suffered from mercury poisoning, as researchers detected toxic amounts of the poison on his moustache hairs. Either way, when you've got to go, you've got to go!

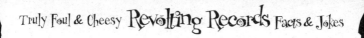

POP!

Death by cackles

In 1660 Sir Thomas Urquhart (an eccentric Scottish writer) laughed himself into an early grave. He must have died happy because he was a great supporter of King Charles I and then later for King Charles II, when there was a civil war to get rid of the royals. When King Charles I was beheaded (no, he didn't laugh his head off), Sir Thomas was very upset (but not as upset as King Charles). England had no real king for a while and Sir Thomas wasn't happy.

But then he heard that King Charles II was safely on the throne and everything seemed super. Thomas was so thrilled that he dropped dead in a fit of 'excessive laughter'. So just be careful if you laugh too much at any of the jokes in this book (unlikely!).

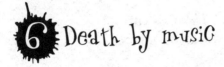

6 Death by music

A famous French composer called Jean-Baptiste Lully (1632-1687) killed himself when conducting an orchestra too enthusiastically. He used a large stick to beat time by bashing it on the floor but, unfortunately, he got his foot in the way and CRUNCH! His wounded foot became infected with gangrene and he refused to have his foot amputated, so he died from blood poisoning. It wasn't a very harmonious end.

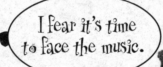

I fear it's time to face the music.

7 Death by makeup

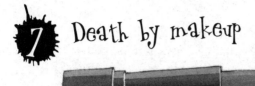

Throughout the 17th and 18th centuries, ladies of fashion used white makeup and arsenic powder to improve their beauty – but not their health. In the 1750s Maria Gunning (Lady Coventry) was something of a celebrity, particularly as she spent a lot of time making herself look beautiful. That meant wearing white makeup and bright red rouge every day.

Her husband tried to stop her from using so much makeup but she wouldn't listen. She should have done, because at the age of 27 she died from overuse of lead-based makeup. She and others killed themselves by trying to look cool and 'drop dead gorgeous'. It worked!

8 Death by extra helpings

A king of Sweden called Adolph Frederick (1710–1771) became known as 'the king who ate himself to death' because he ended up with a massive stomach ache after eating a giant meal consisting of lobster, caviar, sauerkraut, cabbage soup, smoked herring, champagne and 14 servings of his favourite dessert: semla, a bun filled with marzipan and warm milk. Some say he got his just desserts!

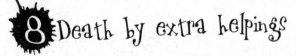

I'm dying for my dinner!

9 Death by arrogance

John Sedgewick has gone down in history's record books for his famous last words, which turned out to be rather foolish.

During the American Civil War, this Union Army general was leading troops at a battle in 1864. Striding out into heavy fire, he was reported to tell his soldiers there was nothing to be worried about as the enemy was miles away: 'They couldn't hit an elephant at this dist...' Whereupon a bullet hit him in the head and he dropped dead.

OOPS.

 Death by silliness

In 1871 an American lawyer called Clement Vallandigham was trying to defend a man in court who was charged with shooting someone. Vallandigham wanted to convince the jury that the victim could have shot himself by accident.

He grabbed what he thought was an unloaded pistol and began to demonstrate what might have happened. The gun went off, and a bullet went into Vallandigham's chest. He proved his point and his client was cleared but Vallandigham was no more!

Limerick

A limerick for anyone wanting
to go in the 'Death Files':

If you pass out and start
somersaulting
Or your breathing appears to be
halting,
You might be expiring...
But the news is inspiring...
You'll go down in these records
marked 'Revolting'.

Famous at the end

Many people live ordinary lives and their details never get recorded unless they die in bizarre ways. Here are just six people who met nasty ends, which got them in the record books forever.

How revolting can you get?

1

In 1912 an Austrian tailor made himself a special cape that he claimed could make him fly. Franz Reichelt was so convinced that his invention would enable him to glide above Paris that he wore it at the top of the Eiffel Tower... then jumped off. Sadly, his cape didn't work and he dropped to his death. He ended up as a splat in the history books for all the wrong reasons.

It's not so much Eiffel as 'I fell'!

2

Many people try to live long lives by eating healthily. Some take extra vitamins in the hope they might break the record to become the longest living human. That record is currently held by Jeanne Calment of France, who lived to the grand old age of 122 years 164 days. Born in 1875, she witnessed the building of the Eiffel Tower and finally died in 1997. She claimed that olive oil kept her healthy.

A year before Jeanne died, an Englishman called Basil Brown swallowed extra vitamins in the hope of making himself super-healthy. Over 10 days he took about 10,000 times the recommended dose of vitamin A, and drank about 10 gallons of carrot juice. That's far too much vitamin A and he died of severe liver damage. His skin was bright yellow.

Had he read the record books, he would have known the dangers of vitamin A poisoning. Long ago, people in the Arctic who hunted polar bears to eat their livers died from the massive amount of vitamin A inside the bears. So, a word of warning: never eat polar bear liver with extra carrots!

Keep your hands off my liver.

3 What is the foulest, most disgusting way you can imagine to die? A woman mayor in the USA sadly found out in 1980. Monica Meyer, the mayor of Betterton, Maryland, decided to check the town's sewage tanks and fell right in. She drowned in 5 metres of human waste. It was like thick smelly putty which sucked her down like quicksand. Many newspapers recorded her revolting end.

4 A Canadian man entered the 'bizarre deaths' record books in 1993. Garry Hoy, a 38-year-old lawyer in Toronto, was trying to prove the windows of a skyscraper were unbreakable. In front of several people, he threw himself against the glass and, as usual, he rebounded harmlessly. When Hoy threw himself against the pane a second time, it popped out of its frame and sent him tumbling 24 stories to his death below.

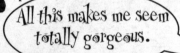

All this makes me seem totally gorgeous.

5 Some people try to enter the record books by eating disgusting things. In 2012, 32-year-old Edward Archbold swallowed dozens of cockroaches and worms in a competition in Florida. Between 20 and 30 contestants were taking part to see who could eat the most bugs. The gross feast proved too much for Edward and he collapsed within minutes and died. Instead of winning a prize, he ended up in the record books under 'death by cockroach'. It's best to avoid eating bugs if you can!

27

3
CHEESY
JOKES
from the cheesiest record books

Did you hear about the man who tried to get into the record books by eating 100 daffodil bulbs? He was rushed to hospital in a bad way. Doctors say that he's now recovering in a raised bed and should be out in the spring. (Warning – don't eat daffodil bulbs, they're very poisonous!)

Old prison records describe how a chemist, a shopkeeper and a teacher were sentenced to death by firing squad. The chemist was taken from his cell and as the soldiers took aim he shouted 'Avalanche!' The soldiers panicked and in the confusion the chemist escaped. Next the shopkeeper was led out, and as the soldiers took aim, he shouted 'Flood!'.

The soldiers panicked and in the confusion the shopkeeper escaped. Finally, the teacher was led out. The squad took aim and the teacher, remembering how the other two had escaped, shouted 'Fire!'.

Whoever recorded these jokes should be shot.

Apparently, the next joke has been voted the funniest in surveys. You decide if you agree!

> There's nothing wrong with my lovely baby.

> Then there must be something wrong with your eyes.

Do you think I look revolting?

No - but you smell it!

A woman gets on a bus with her baby. The bus driver says: 'Ugh, that's the ugliest baby I've ever seen!' The woman walks to the rear of the bus and sits down, fuming. She says to a man next to her: 'The driver just insulted me. I'm so upset.' The man says: 'You go up there and tell him off. Go on, and I'll hold your monkey for you.'

Just plane scary

Brace yourself for a bumpy ride. The record books are full of daring parachute jumps from the highest or fastest free fall jumps to amazing stories of survival when parachutes fail. But what about falling from an aircraft without a parachute at all? Here are just three reports of amazing young females who were record-breaking survivors.

RUMBLE

On Christmas Eve in 1971, 17-year-old Juliane Köpcke was among over 90 people on a flight over Peru, with the Amazon jungle far below. Suddenly a terrible thunderstorm struck and the plane broke up in mid-air. All the aircraft's 6 crew and 85 of its 86 passengers fell to their deaths.

Juliane was the only survivor, falling 2 miles down into the Amazon rainforest strapped to her seat. Trees broke her fall and the next morning she awoke on the jungle floor. Injured and alone, she staggered through the jungle, trying to find water. She knew she needed to find a river and hopefully get to a village along its banks.

Get me my
dinner – and make it
snappy.

Juliane waded from tiny streams
to larger ones. She passed snapping
crocodiles and poked the mud in front of
her with a stick to scare away dangerous
creatures. With only one shoe and
wearing a ripped miniskirt, she plodded
on through the sweltering rainforest. Her
only food was a bag of sweets and she
had nothing but muddy water to drink.
She ignored her broken collarbone and
her wounds, which became infested with
maggots. Flies laid eggs under her skin
and she tried to dig them out of her flesh.

34

After 10 days and getting weaker each day, she saw a canoe tethered to a riverbank. It took her hours to climb the embankment to a hut, where, the next day, a group of lumberjacks found her. Eventually she was treated in hospital and lived to tell her incredible story, which has gone down in the survival books as one of the most remarkable on record.

SNAP!

All-time record breaker

The following year, in 1972, another young woman was the only survivor of a plane crash in the Czech Republic. 23-year-old Vesna Vulovic was an air steward when an explosion tore the DC-9 she was working aboard to pieces in mid-air. Against all the odds, she survived a fall from 10,160 metres. That's over 6 miles up in the sky! She was in hospital for 16 months after emerging from a 27-day coma and having many bones broken. Vesna died in 2016, aged 66, but still holds the Guinness world record for surviving the highest fall ever without a parachute.

Miracle

In 2009, 14-year-old French schoolgirl Bahia Bakari became world famous as the sole survivor of an Airbus A310, which crashed into the Indian Ocean, killing all other 152 people on board. Bahia couldn't swim and had no lifejacket, but she managed to cling to aircraft wreckage in heavy seas for more than 13 hours, much of it in pitch darkness.

She was eventually seen from a rescue ship and was thrown a lifebelt, but the sea was too rough and she was too exhausted to grab it. One of the sailors jumped in to save her and she eventually recovered from her scary ordeal, being named 'The Miracle Girl' by the world's press.

Skydiving nightmare
(don't read this if you ever plan to go for a parachute jump!)

In 1993, Frenchman Didier Dahran parachuted over France but at 300 metres from the ground, a freak storm sucked him back up into the clouds. He shot up to 10,000 metres where it was 30 degrees below freezing. The icy wind kept him at that height for two hours before his parachute collapsed and he fell like a stone. Although he almost passed out, Didier managed to pull his spare parachute just in time. He landed safely 30 miles away, suffering from frostbite and shock, but relieved to survive.

A similar nightmare happened in 2002 when Mathieu Gagnon was sucked into a dark storm cloud while parachuting in Ontario, Canada. He was pulled up by the storm and, after rising 1,000 metres, he cut away his main parachute and fell out of the clouds. Using his reserve parachute, he came down over 15 miles from the airfield where he was supposed to land.

A plane silly joke

A plane was flying high over the mountains, with just four people on board – the pilot, a young boy scout, a nun and a professor of world records. During the flight the pilot came back and said that they were experiencing engine difficulties and that the plane was going to crash. The good news was that they had parachutes, but the bad news was that there were only three.

I am on record as being a complete genius.

This is utter NUNsense!

Explaining that he had to make a full report of the situation to the authorities, the pilot quickly put on a parachute and jumped. There were now three people left on the diving plane and just two parachutes.

The professor stood up next and explained that he had studied at Oxford, Harvard, Yale and other such universities, and that he was one of the most intelligent people in the world. He said that the world needed his wisdom and great learning. So, he grabbed a parachute and jumped.

The nun considered her age and that she had lived a full life and was ready to face her last seconds. She told the boy that he should use the last parachute. The boy scout smiled and said calmly, 'Don't worry, we'll both be fine. The most intelligent person in the world just put on my backpack before he jumped.'

The Toilet Files

Even toilets appear in the record books. After all, the history of toilets is a big (no, not bog) subject. That 'little room' has often been the place of high drama.

Dying to go to the bathroom

King George II of Great Britain died on his toilet in 1760. According to the official record, King George 'rose as usual at six, and drank his chocolate; for all his actions were invariably methodic. A quarter after seven he went into a little closet. His German valet de chambre in waiting heard a noise, and running in, found the King dead on the floor.'

The report doesn't record if he felt pooped or flushed.

You just don't want to know some of the records kept in the 'Toilet Files'...

TOILET BOWL SNAKE ATTACKS ON THE RISE
(according to statistics in the USA)

The Federal Bureau of Statistics recorded in 1997 that there were 105 reported toilet bowl snake attacks. Not everyone who was bitten on their bottom survived to visit the bathroom again. In 1998, there were 135 attacks and in 1999, 200 attacks were reported. Why? Apparently, the increase of new homes in 'snake country' has disturbed natural reptile habitats. 'Until new serpent-proof toilets and plumbing are developed, this problem is going to get worse and worse out in the suburbs,' an expert reported.

Look out

– it gets worse...

Stories of snakes coming up drains and toilet pipes are quite common, according to Queensland Wildlife Solutions in Australia, a snake-catching business in Brisbane.

Snakes in sewers give me goosebumps.

Apparently, snakes follow the trail of rats. 'All over the world, rats go down in sewers and the snakes go in there after them. And from there they can find your bathroom,' said a snake-catcher who gets called out to remove at least five snakes from toilets each year – usually green tree snakes, common tree snakes or carpet pythons.

'It's the worst job. You get a toilet bowl that's been there 30 or 40 years – we see the bit that gets cleaned but the rest of it doesn't. When you go to pull the thing out of there, it's not fun. I usually have a bottle of disinfectant with me,' he says. 'You've got to grab the head or whatever you can get hold of and start dragging it out.'

Yikes – don't have too many nightmares!

Would you like a seat?

Riddle time

Q: What do you do if you find a black mamba in your toilet? (That's one of the deadliest things on the planet... the snake, not your toilet!)
A: Wait until it's finished.

Q: How do you know if you've got snakes living in your bathroom?
A: The bath towels are marked 'Hiss and Hers'.

Q: What subject do snakes like best at school?
A: Hiss-tory (especially the hiss-tory of toiletssssss).

47

A revolting limerick

Next time that you sit on the loo
Be prepared for a snake rendezvous...
Plopping up from below
For a hissing 'hello',
And a beady-eyed hullabaloo.
(Don't worry – the government is
looking into toilets with specially
trained civil serpents.)

While on the subject of snakes...

An enormous python measuring 8 metres long was captured on a Malaysian building site in 2016, but it died three days later while laying an egg. The Malaysian snake was said to be longer than five grand pianos or as long as an adult giraffe standing on the head of another giraffe!

This snake was longer than Medusa, the longest captive snake on record. In 2011, Medusa, also a python, measured 7.67 metres at her home in Kansas City, Missouri, Guinness World Records reported. Let's hope she doesn't escape down the drain and pop up in a toilet near you!

Criminal Records

The record books are full of revolting crime records that will make your toes curl and even drop off. Try some of these execution figures to make you squirm…

- From 1484 until 1750 about 200,000 people thought to be witches were tortured, burned or hanged in Western Europe. Most of these victims were usually poor, old women who were often sunken-cheeked with a hairy lip and assumed to possess the 'Evil Eye'. If they lived alone and owned a cat this was usually enough proof to get them executed. The last woman to be hanged as a witch in England was Alice Mollard, in 1686.

• According to some records, during the reign of King Henry VIII, which lasted 38 years from 1509 to 1547, 72,000 people were executed for one crime or another.

• During the French Revolution, between May 1792 and June 1793 when the French were revolting, 1,255 people had their heads sliced off by the guillotine in Paris.

Keep quiet or we'll get it in the neck!

51

• Joseph Samuel was sentenced to be hanged in Australia in 1803. The first attempt failed when the rope broke. The second attempt failed when the new rope stretched so that Samuel's feet touched the ground. At the third attempt, the rope broke again, so Samuel was let off. John Lee also survived three hangings when the trap door failed to open each time in Exeter, UK in 1885. He was kept hanging around for ages!

• The first person ever to be executed by the electric chair was William Kemmler, a murderer, who was electrocuted in 1890 in New York, USA.

• Execution by electric chair isn't always as instant as you might think. In 1922, prisoner James Wells required 11 repeated zaps to electrocute him. Shocking, eh?

53

Records of the body-snatchers

Criminals long ago used to buy and sell dead human bodies. In the 1700s and 1800s, fresh corpses were needed by medical schools for training doctors. Grave-robbers would enter churchyards in the dead of night to dig up fresh corpses – the fresher, the better. But then, in 1827, two men working in Edinburgh took body-snatching to a revoltingly new level.

I've got somebody to take home with me

William Burke and William Hare entered the record books for taking the trade in dead bodies to the extreme. They murdered victims and sold them for medical research. It all started when an old man living in the same lodging house died owing them money, so they decided to sell his body to get their money back. They took the body to Dr Knox's anatomy school and were paid well – no questions asked.

Over the following months, Burke and Hare murdered 15 more people. All their victims were very poor and often homeless. They made a lot of money – until someone reported seeing a body in Burke's bed! Burke and Hare were arrested and, in the first case of its kind, Hare agreed to tell the whole story so he could be let off. Burke was hanged on 28th January 1829 as a record crowd cheered in the streets.

Burke's body was dissected and the next day it was exhibited to over 30,000 members of the public. Burke's skeleton can be found today at the Edinburgh University Museum – as well as a leather-covered notebook made from Burke's skin. How revolting is that?

Limerick

Dr Knox's dissections were
gruesome
Yet crowds would assemble
to view some...
And to see Burke and Hare,
That bloodthirsty pair...
The infamous murderous
twosome.

More criminal records

1 Most arrested

Dennis Payne, aged 30, was
arrested as a pickpocket
in 1993 at a Jersey City
railway station in the
USA, his 135th arrest since
1978. Police said it took
a computer more than
half an hour to print out
Payne's huge arrest record.

2 The longest sentence

A criminal from Oklahoma with a long record of many crimes was given a prison sentence of 2,000 years in 1944. Darron Anderson appealed but received further sentences for each of his crimes. In 1997, he once again appealed the decision and this time had a little more success, as his parole date was set as the year 2744. The length of his prison sentence was now 384,912 years.

This is utter poppycock.

I'll be the judge of that.

3 Even longer

22-year-old postman Gabriel Grandos of Spain went on trial in 1972 for failing to deliver 42,768 letters. The court decided he should receive a sentence of nine years in prison for every lost letter – that's almost 400,000 years in total. In the end, the judge decided to give him a slightly shorter sentence of 14 years and two months, instead. Never had so many letters made such a long sentence!

You want a short sentence? Try this: You're guilty.

This must be good for my skin.

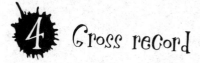

4 Gross record

It's impossible to know for sure who the worst serial killer in history was, but many historians consider it to be the Hungarian Countess, Elizabeth Bathory. This royal lady terrified most people in Hungary during the 1500s. She was dubbed the 'Blood Countess' because she quite liked to bathe in her victims' blood. Historians think this blood-thirsty Hungarian Countess personally murdered around 650 people.

Criminal Jokes

Did you hear about the murderer who attacked people with a large box of cornflakes? He was a cereal killer.

A murderer sitting in the electric chair was about to be executed. 'Have you any last requests?' asked the executioner. 'Yes,' replied the murderer. 'Will you hold my hand?'

What's the difference between a thief and a church bell?
One steals from the people, the other peals from the steeple.

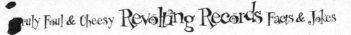

Did you hear about the burglar who fell in the cement mixer?
Now he's a hardened criminal.

Did you hear about the criminal on the run who sawed the legs off his bed?
He decided to lie low for a while.

What do prisoners use to call each other?
Cell phones. (And if they take their own photo in prison it must be a cell-fie!)

If you ask me, this page is criminally cheesy.

A cheesy criminal story

A prisoner received a letter from his wife:

Dear husband, I have decided to plant some lettuce and onions in the back yard so you'll have something to put in a nice cheese sandwich when you get home. When is the best time to plant them?

The prisoner knew the prison guards read all the mail, so he replied with: 'Dear wife, whatever you do, do not touch the back yard. Under all that concrete is where I hid all the money.'

A week or so later, he received another letter from his wife. 'Dear husband, you wouldn't believe what happened. Some men came with picks and shovels to the house and dug up the whole back yard.'

The prisoner wrote back with a smile: 'Dear wife, now is the best time to plant seeds in the back yard. Job done!'

Crazy Creatures

5 Random Animal Records

The giant African land snail can grow to a record-breaking 25 cm long – it's a slimy creature with a hungry mouth that causes great damage to plants. The giant snails have spread around the world, chomping through vegetation as they go. In 1966 a boy in Florida had three of these snails as pets but his grandma released them into the garden. Oops. Seven years later there were 18,000 of the shelled pests eating up Florida and leaving thick slimy trails everywhere. Gross!

Slimy riddle:

What happened when the giant snail lost its shell?
It began to feel sluggish.

2 The fastest time taken to pop 100 balloons by a dog is 44.49 sec by Anastasia (a Jack Russell Terrier) in Los Angeles, USA, in 2008.

SILLY BALLOON JOKE

Daddy balloon said to Baby balloon, 'Look son, you are much too old to sleep with mummy and daddy, you must sleep in your own bed tonight.'

Baby balloon cried, 'But I want to sleep with you and mummy.'

Mummy balloon snapped, 'No, you are not sleeping with us and that's final.'

At two in the morning, Baby balloon woke up and climbed into bed with mummy and daddy. Finding no room, he untied his dad's knot and let out some air, then tied him up again. Still no room, so he untied his mummy's knot, let some air out and tied her up again. There was still no room so Baby balloon untied his own knot, let out some air, then tied himself up again. At last there was room so he snuggled down with mummy and daddy.

The next day they all woke up but Daddy balloon was angry. He said, 'Son, I am really disappointed with you. I told you not to sleep in our bed. You've let me down, you've let mummy down, and what's more, you've really let yourself down.'

3 The most basketball slam dunks by a parrot in one minute was 22, and was achieved by Zac the Macaw in California, USA, in 2011.

Yay - how's that for polly-filla?

Silly parrot riddle

Q: Why did the parrot wear a raincoat?
A: She said she wanted to be Polly unsaturated.

70

 The farthest distance skateboarding by a goat was 36 metres and was achieved by Happie of Florida, USA in 2012. The distance was completed in a time of 25 seconds.

Silly goat riddle

Q: What do you call a goat dressed like a clown on a skateboard on a cold day?
A: A chilly silly billy.

 The fastest crossing of a tightrope by a dog was 18.22 seconds and was achieved by Ozzy (a Border Collie/Kelpie cross) in 2013 in Norfolk, UK.

Silly tightrope joke

Q: Why did the tightrope walker visit the bank?
A: He wanted to check his balance.

Worrying Wolf Records

Stories and legends of hungry wolves have scared people for thousands of years, but do wolves really deserve their scary reputation? These three tales from the records might well give you nightmares...

I don't believe you - you're crying wolf.

In the winter of 1450, the wolves near Paris were starving because humans had cut into their forest habitat and hunted their food. So the starving wolves crept through holes in the city walls. At first, they raided livestock, but they soon became bolder. A pack led by a red wolf with a bobbed tail went right into the city and attacked. They devoured 40 people, savaging women and children.

When the wolves came back days later, the people were ready. A mob chased them until they were at the front of the Cathedral of Notre Dame. There, the people gathered up stones and threw them, stoning the animals to death. No wonder stories of hungry wolves have become part of ancient folklore and legends.

In 1911, a Russian wedding turned into something more like from a horror movie than a celebration. A total of 120 people had gathered in the village of Obstipoff for the ceremony. When the service ended, they prepared for the 20-mile journey to the banquet. It was to be a romantic ride, with horse-driven sleighs carrying the party through the snow.

Do you remember Little Red Riding Hood?

But after they set off, the horses became nervous. The party was being followed... Then the wedding guests saw what looked like a huge black shadow growing on a snowy hill. Soon they realized what it was: hundreds of frenzied wolves charging straight at them. Every man, woman and child in the rear sleighs was attacked and eaten. The ones at the front pushed forward, but one by one, the wolves overtook them.

Soon, only the bridal sleigh was left, with the bride, the groom, and two other men on board. Their only hope, the two men said later, was to throw the bride to the wolves. Her newlywed husband tried to protect her, but he, too, was devoured alive. Apparently only two men survived what became known as the worst wolf attack in history.

According to the Guinness Book of Records, the largest pack of wolves went on the prowl in the winter of 2010-11. A 'super pack' of wolves numbering up to 400 reportedly terrorized the small Russian town of Verkhoyansk in a remote region. More than 30 horses were killed in just four days, according to local officials, and teams of hunters had to guard the townspeople.

However, it is very rare for
wolves to form packs much
larger than 15 animals.
So fear not... hungry wolf
packs may have attacked
in the past but surely not
nooooooowwwwwwwwwwwwwwwwwwwww.

These jokes are even
too cheesy for me!

The Baked Tapioca Flood

Tapioca is a gooey, stodgy, splodgy milky pudding made from chewy small pearls of starch from cassava root. In 1972 a firefighter had to tackle what he called 'A huge tapioca time bomb,' when a cargo ship caught fire at sea.

The ship was stocked with timber and tapioca sacks which were smouldering badly as it docked in a Welsh harbour. Firefighters sprayed their hoses onto the smoking ship but the water ran down inside to the ship's lower levels, where 1,500 tons of tapioca were stored. The tapioca expanded from the heat and the water, and the flaming ship was in danger of bursting in a giant helping of piping hot tapioca pudding. Luckily, the fire was put out just before the biggest ever tapioca splurge could happen. Phew!

THE PIG MANURE FLOOD

What could be worse than being up to your neck in a bubbling wave of liquid pig dung? Maybe being up to your eyebrows would be worse. In 2006 a torrent of pig muck struck the German village of Elsa when a massive tank storing liquefied pig excrement burst open. Almost 53,000 gallons (250,000 litres) of greenish-brown stinking slop flooded the Bavarian village, quickly becoming more than half a metre deep in revolting pig sludge, which flooded several homes. Villagers were pig-sick and kicked up a mighty stink with the nincomPOOPS in charge.

They'll never clean this up - it's all hogwash!

The Octopus Flood

When an octopus escaped from its tank one night in 2009, it used one of its tentacles to tug open a valve at the Santa Monica Pier Aquarium. The fiddling creature released hundreds of gallons of water, which gushed out over the floor, along with lots of flapping fish. The next morning the aquarium staff arrived to find their offices flooded, but they managed to rescue all the stranded sea creatures in time. At first, they thought something dead fishy was going on – till they discovered the culprit giggling. After all, octopuses are quite ticklish and this one was wriggling from ten tickles (tentacles).

Silly riddles for octopuses

I'm a sucker for you.

You octopi all my thoughts.

Q: Who stole the baby octopus and held it to ransom?
A: Squidnappers

Q: What did the boy octopus say to the girl octopus?
A: I wanna hold your hand, hand, hand, hand, hand, hand, hand, hand!

Q: What's wet and wiggly and says 'how do you do?' sixteen times?
A: Two octopuses shaking hands.

Randomly revolting and revoltingly random

Some people try all sorts of weird, gross and daft things just to get in the record books.

How about these 12 randomly revolting records?

1 1998
Kim Goodman from Chicago popped
her eyeballs 11 mm beyond her eye
sockets on the TV show Guinness
World Records Primetime. Don't try it!

2 1999
Gary Bashaw set the record for the
most milkshake squirted through the
nose when milk and chocolate powder
came out of his nostrils on the set of a
Guinness World Records TV programme
in Los Angeles. Why would you do that?

3 1999
John LaMedica of Delaware, USA, lay in
a coffin and had 20,050 giant Madagascan
hissing cockroaches poured over him on
the TV show Guinness World Records
Primetime. The cockroaches probably
found the experience truly revolting!

This stuff really
bugs me.

4 2000

American Mark Hogg swallowed a total of 94 worms in 30 seconds on a TV programme. Why didn't he just stay at home and eat spaghetti instead?

5 2001

Smudge, a parrot, set a record for the most keys removed from a keyring by a parrot by slipping off 10 in under two minutes. In 2009, he got all the way up to 22. He's certainly worked out the key to a good record.

Don't try this at home!

I'm bursting to beat the record.

6 2004

Chad Fell blew the largest bubblegum bubble on record, at over 50 cm in diameter, at the Double Springs High School in Alabama, USA. That must have been way bigger than his own head!

7 2006

An Indian man in his eighties clocked up 50 years of sitting up a tree after a row with his wife. Gayadhar Parida took to staying in a mango tree after a quarrel, but he had to change trees when his first tree was destroyed in a storm. Mr Parida's tree in Orissa was home to poisonous snakes, yet he only came down to drink water from a pool. His son brought him food and begged his father to return home – to no avail. Was it also his lava-tree?

8 2006

Since first receiving a skin piercing in 1997, Elaine Davidson (Brazil/UK) has been pierced a total of 4,225 times. She constantly adds jewellery through the piercings, mostly in her face – as well as having tattoos and brightly coloured makeup, with feathers and streamers in her hair. She must like to be noticed!

9 2008

Kevin Shelley set the record for the most toilet seats broken by his head in one minute by shattering 46 in Cologne, Germany. The mind BOGgles!

10 2009

Melvin Boothe had the longest fingernails for a male ever at 983 cm when they were measured in Troy, Michigan. His record certainly came up to scratch.

A German woman owns a record 47,000 rat-related items such as rat Toby jugs. What a mug!

11 2009

Fin Keleher from Utah, USA, had to keep 43 live snails on his head and face for 10 seconds to break the world record. The 11-year-old set out to break the previous record during a party to celebrate his birthday. At the party, with help from his family, Fin managed to keep 43 snails on his face. Some snails thought it was a cheek.

HIS

I may be cold-blooded but I've got a warm poisonality.

S SS

12 2009

Jackie Bibby, 'The Texas Snake Man', gained the record of holding 11 full-grown rattle snakes in his mouth by their rattling tails for 10 seconds. He then spat them out and dashed away without being bitten. However, he's been bitten other times and later lost a leg from a poisoned snake bite. It's probably best not to try breaking that record!

SCARY
Statistics

What is the chance of getting eaten by a shark later today? The answer is zilch if you live far from the sea (unless you go to Sea World and fall in the aquarium). Seeing as very few people are killed by sharks in a year (on average just five people worldwide), you should be safe at the swimming baths.

Apparently, according to National Geographic, you have a 1 in 3,700,000 chance of being killed by a shark during your lifetime but a 1 in 63 chance of dying from the flu. And it's an even slimmer chance of being attacked by a shark with flu!

The experts who work on probability (that's the chance of something happening) have worked out how likely it is for the 'average person' to die from different things. The problem with such statistics is that few people are strictly average. A lot depends on who you are, your lifestyle and where you live. If you're American, these are supposed to be your chances of meeting a sudden death:

'Odds of dying in selected events in the USA: 1 in...

112: MOTOR VEHICLE ACCIDENT

358: ASSAULT WITH FIREARM

8,015: PLANE CRASH

42,120: VENOMOUS ANIMAL/PLANT

164,968: LIGHTNING

3.1 million: SHARK ATTACK

NOT AGAIN

Although the risk of being killed by lightning is very low, one estimate is that 24,000 people are killed by lightning strikes around the world each year and about 240,000 are injured.

Some people are just unlucky... The only man in the world to be struck by lightning seven times was ex-park ranger Roy Sullivan, the human lightning conductor of Virginia, USA. He was first struck by lightning in 1942. He survived but lost a big toe nail. Next time was in 1969 when lightning scorched off his eyebrows. The next year lightning burnt his left shoulder and in 1972 another strike set his hair on fire. His hair went up again next strike, then in 1976 his ankle was struck. Finally, in 1977, his chest and stomach were burnt.

Maybe being a park ranger is high risk – that's probably why he went on strike!

Joke time

During a violent thunderstorm, a lightning bolt struck a tree in the garden just as a mother was tucking her small boy into bed. When the loud crack finally died down, she went to turn off the light as her petrified son whimpered, 'Mummy, will you sleep in my bed tonight?'

His mother smiled and gave him a reassuring hug. 'I can't dear,' she said. 'I have to sleep in Daddy's room. Be brave, love.'

96

The boy gave a shaky
sigh and whispered,
'Okay – but that man
is such a big wimp.'

Lightning is so
reVOLTing.

Things to avoid if you want to survive the rest of today

What unusual things kill many humans each year? Forget sharks and take note...

Next time you go to a theme park, take a good look at the roller coaster. Although the risk of injury while riding a roller coaster is very low, the average death rate in the USA is four people per year. Americans take about 900 million rides per year, yet only about 1 in 124,000 result in an injury. From 1994-2004 there were 40 deaths from roller coasters, so that put the annual death rate at four per year in the USA.

After that rollercoaster ride I feel sick...

Death by snacks

Next time you kick a vending machine for not delivering a chocolate bar – take care!

Each year vending machines topple over and crush about 10-13 people to death. That's more than the number of people killed by shark attacks. Over 1,700 injuries are recorded from vending machines each year in the USA alone.

Even so, someone with not much to do worked out that you are 10 times more likely to die if you're attacked by a shark than if you're attacked by a vending machine. NEVER try to get a shark out of a vending machine… just in case.

I didn't ANTicipate this lot!

Death by ants

Did you know there are many different species of ants that can kill us? The fire ant and Siafu ants of Africa are among the deadliest if they all bite or sting at once. As they can live in colonies of up to 20 million, once an attack begins, ants easily overpower their prey. Most reports of deaths are due to people falling asleep near an ant hill and suffering major shock from bites and venom. Up to 30 people a year could die from such intolerANTS!

Death by jellyfish

20 to 40 people die from stings by box jellyfish each year in the Philippines alone, according to the U.S. National Science Foundation. But that figure could be much higher worldwide – making jellyfish far deadlier than sharks. Jellyfish stings cause deaths most years in Australia (where box jellyfish have caused more than 60 deaths over the last 100 years).

Death from above

Sharp blades of ice falling from above are blamed for killing 100 people per year in Russia alone. Each year dozens are killed when pointed icicles fall from snowy rooftops and land on them in the streets below. So, you're more likely to be attacked by ice than a shark in Russia.

Death in the bedroom

Can you believe that falling out of bed is said to kill 450 people each year in the USA?

According to the Centre for Disease Control, falling out of bed accounts for 1.8 million emergency room visits and over 400 thousand hospital admissions each year. The very young and the very old are most at risk from rolling over in bed and CRASH! The trouble with going to bed is that you can soon drop off.

EEEK

Africa's deadliest?

Hippos are the third largest land mammal, after the elephant and the rhinoceros. Although they are vegetarians, hippos can kill crocodiles and apparently harm more people in Africa each year than are killed by lions and leopards.

I may look cuddly but watch out!

SNAP!

Many experts believe the hippopotamus is the most dangerous animal in all of Africa, with an estimate that they kill about 2,900 people each year. Able to gallop at 20 mph, they can upset boats and bite the passengers with their massive teeth. Not only that, but hippos are aggressive, unpredictable and have no fear of humans. People die most often when they get between a hippo and deep water or between a mother and her calf. If a hippo tries to tell you otherwise, it's a **HIPPOcrite!**

Joke records

How would you like to beat the world record for the number of cheesy jokes told in one minute? All you have to do is time yourself reading from this book! The number to beat is 26 jokes in 60 seconds (that's less than 2.5 seconds per joke!). The current record was set by Clive Greenaway from Dorset, UK in 2015. Most of his jokes were fast one-liners like this...

'Today I ate a ploughman's lunch – he wasn't happy. I went to the paper shop – but it blew away.'

In 2002 almost two million people from 70 countries voted on their favourite jokes. The winner went like this:

A couple of New Jersey hunters are out in the woods when one of them falls to the ground. He doesn't seem to be breathing and his eyes have rolled back in his head.

The other guy whips out his mobile phone and calls the emergency services. He gasps to the operator: 'My friend is dead! What can I do?'

The operator, in a soothing voice, says: 'Just take it easy. I can help. First, let's make sure he's dead.'

There is a silence, then a shot is heard. The guy's voice comes back on the line. He says: 'OK, now what?'

I've just read a horror story - it's your medical record.

Apparently, people from Britain, Ireland, Australia and New Zealand preferred jokes involving word play like this:

Patient: 'Doctor, I've got a strawberry stuck up my very sore nose.'

Doctor: 'I've got some cream for that.'

Americans and Canadians liked jokes where a person was made to look stupid:

Texan: 'Where are you from?'

Harvard graduate: 'Actually, I come from a place where we do not end our sentences with a preposition.'

Texan: 'Ok, where are you from, idiot?'

For the record, don't mess with Texas, buddy.

Sure thing, cowboy.

Many European countries,
such as France, Denmark and
Belgium, enjoyed jokes that
were wacky, such as:

An Alsatian dog went to a
telegram office and wrote: 'Woof.
Woof. Woof. Woof. Woof. Woof.
Woof. Woof. Woof.'

The clerk examined the
paper and told the dog:
'There are only nine words
here. You could send another
'Woof' for the same price.'

'But,' the dog replied, 'that
would make no sense at all.'

And finally...

The Cheesiest Records ever

Five Italian chefs made the World's Biggest Pizza in Rome in 2012. The deliciously round monstrosity measured 40 metres in diameter. Just imagine a plate that size! It tipped the scales at over 23,000 kg, and contained 675 kg of margarine, nearly 9,000 kg of flour, 4,500 kg of tomato sauce and almost 4,000 kg of mozzarella cheese. It didn't quite fit in a box but was stored in a massive warehouse.

Cheesy pizza joke

As soon as the customer opened the pizza box, he sneezed uncontrollably. He asked the delivery man, 'Whatever did you put on this pizza?'. The delivery man said, 'We put on that pizza just what you ordered – pepper only.' (Pepperoni, get it?)

The biggest commercially available hamburger in the world consists of 7 kg of lettuce, 14 kg of bacon, 14 kg of tomatoes and 16 kg of cheese. It takes around 22 hours to make and it is available with a portion of fries and a drink. A large crowd gathered to dribble over the unveiling of this $2,000 menu item in 2011 at Mallie's Sports Grill & Bar of Southgate, Michigan, USA. At a metre high and packing 540,000 calories, this is the largest hamburger you can buy, according to World Record Academy.

Cheesy burger joke

What do you call 5 dolls in a row waiting for a large cheeseburger?
A Barbie-queue

[If you survived the truly foul facts and cheesy jokes in this book, take a look at the other mad titles in this revolting series. They're all guaranteed to make you groan and squirm like never before. You have been warned!]

QUIZ

1. Who died of 'excessive laughter' in 1660?

a) Sir William Giggle-a-lot

b) Lady Cynthia Chuckles

c) Sir Thomas Urquhart

2. How many basketball slam dunks did Zac the Macaw make in one minute in 2011?

a) 22

b) 20

c) 24

3. How many people were tortured or executed as witches in Western Europe from 1484 to 1750?

a) 200,000

b) 500,000

c) 1,000,000

You've got to laugh at all this twaddle.

I've never known such cheesy balderdash!

4. Where did King George
II of Great Britain die?

a) In bed

b) On the toilet

c) In the bath

5. How many people are killed by lightning strikes each year?

a) 24,000

b) 30,000

c) 15

6. Who were William Burke and William Hare?

a) The village idiot and a rabbit breeder

b) The body snatchers

c) Highway robbers

The awful thing is ... there are lots more revolting books in this series!

7. What did Elizabeth Bathory like to bathe in?

a) Tomato juice

b) Raw sewage

c) Her victims' blood

8. How many rattlesnakes did Jackie Bibby manage to hold in his mouth?

a) 10

b) 11

c) 8

9. In what year was the first execution by electric chair?

a) 1890

b) 1900

c) 2001

10. What is the third largest land mammal?

a) Hippopotamus

b) Rhino

c) Cow

Answers:

1 = c
2 = a
3 = a
4 = b
5 = a
6 = b
7 = c
8 = b
9 = a
10 = a

It may look like I'm laughing at the jokes. I'M NOT.

GLOSSARY

Amazon: a river and large rainforest in the northern part of South America.

Arsenic: a chemical element that can be found in many minerals and is poisonous to humans.

French Revolution: the period in France between 1787 and 1799 when the middle classes and peasantry rose up against the monarchy and toppled it, killing many members of the aristocracy.

Gangrene: when parts of a living person's body begin to die and decompose because the circulation of blood has been stopped or a bacterial infection has occurred.

Mercury: a metal which exists in a liquid state at room temperature and is poisonous to humans.

Mozzarella: a white cheese made from cow or buffalo milk and typically used as a topping on pizzas.

Vikings: a seafaring race of people from Scandinavia who traded, pillaged and conquered throughout Europe in the 8th-11th centuries.

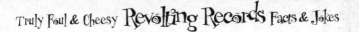

INDEX

I finished reading this Truly
Foul & Cheesy book on:

............/............/............